T0114611

# *Sorrows at*
# Twilight Shores

—— I Wrote to Thee ——

## PROSE WRITINGS

Ahmed Balhamar

authorHOUSE®

*AuthorHouse™*
*1663 Liberty Drive*
*Bloomington, IN 47403*
*www.authorhouse.com*
*Phone: 833-262-8899*

*Published by AuthorHouse  03/06/2023*

*ISBN: 979-8-8230-0253-0 (sc)*
*ISBN: 979-8-8230-0254-7 (hc)*
*ISBN: 979-8-8230-0252-3 (e)*

*Print information available on the last page.*

*This book is printed on acid-free paper.*

# Preface

It is always the case with writing in all its genres, whether prose or poetry, that while many people read it, the meaning is inevitably one.

You are free to reflect on what I have written on my ego ("me"), and you are free to forget me and let the words do their task, and to transfer your seats to others whom I have never invited.

# Longing

Swiftly time passes.
Sometimes I am sitting, sometimes standing, and another time
    fiddling with my leaves and books,
But time stops violently, from which comes the rising smoke of
    longing and waiting.
At that time, I remember I will hear your voice no more, not today
    or even tomorrow.

# soil (1)

I behold the soil in terror and fear,
Sometimes in longing.
My brunette fingers care for its particles; they steep from my palm
    gently and smoothly.
Were it not for those around me, I would put down my forehead
    and nose to taste it.
For from soil am I, and to soil will I be.

# → 3 ←

# soil (2)

Despair and fatigue brought me to what I am; it may be also
  because of my closeness to it.
When I come closer and put my forehead on the soil,
It reminds me of him; he is also made of these small atoms—
Of which, when I raise my head, some stay on my face.

# Writing

I was writing for you, and people testify to that—
All people.
And now I write for myself,
For the people still testify that I am writing.

# My Lost One

I will bury the remains of love, and for it I will build a shrine in a
   place unknown except by me.
I pay a visit to my lost one.
I pay him homage.
I will build for him a tombstone, and then I will go.
I walk apace, then look back so I cannot forget the dwelling place,
Hoping I will pay him a passing visit soon.
The status of my passed one will never change, so I let him do
   what he wants, for he became free
And is released from my slavery and imprisonment to his new
   world.
All existence and eminence are to him, while all things are
   passing by.

# Parting

When I felt it was the parting,
When I got that news
In that place where I used to share my feelings,
At my usual street, the red sidewalks, the highlighted spots, even
   the accumulated dust here and there,
I prostrated before them all, aware of none but me.
At that time I felt it was necessary to unload the last high charge,
Though I had no objection to share with them, since they are my
   friends now.
I prostrated on the sidewalk, for we should thank God in ecstasy
   and agony.
These atoms never let me easily.
When I straightened, they remained on my forehead to please me,
Though I didn't see them but left them to honor them.
Only time can prove to me whether that parting is a grace or a
   curse.
Strangely, I want it as I want.

# Friends of Mine

How are you, friends?
My friend, the straight street;
My friend, the good sidewalk;
My friend, the light spot—
I know you are bored of my frequent complaining,
My sterile condition.
Let us change places.
I will listen while you complain and talk.
I will not interrupt; take your share today. you will rewarded for
    your patience.
I know I will not equal you in sight and care—especially you,
    Muneer.
I cared not for those who are too good and straight intentionally,
But because of my closeness to them and my complaints when a
    hug touches me,
A closer one wipes my reckonings and makes it easy.
As for the looks, the heavy burdens pressed me.
If I forget, you would make me remember to look up and
    exchange looks with you.

# Division

Am I the only one skillful in mathematics?
In addition, subtraction, division, and multiplication?
Or is there someone the same as me in that he collects, counts,
and adds hours to hours and days to days?
So I stop and lose craftsmanship in this skillfulness.
My talents stop these days, but I get worried when I behold that
time exceeds twenty-four hours and enters a new day.
I neither know nor want to reach a month,
Because it is a number that exceeds my capacity and my
comprehension of the mathematical processes,
And if I would reach it, the month, I would change its name and
name it differently—
A name that equals the heartburn and pain, that was caused by
counting these days—or I would stop counting and start
anew every time,
Every time,
Every time.

# → 9 ←

# Escape

My feelings jostled to get out of me—
They piled up and accumulated at the outlets.
They quarreled and fought; the domain is for the one that gets out
first
From my eye,
My fingers,
My foot,
Or my hand.
All will get out.
Be patient, for I patiently gathered them for about a year with
kindness and with great love.
I know that the loud explosion frightened you and made you
crowd to get out.
All of you will get out on time.
And all of you will get out as his image.

# Untitled

What is the treatment that restores feeling and sensation to the
   five fingers of my hand?
I no longer feel warm when I touch any skin
Or when I shake hands with someone.
It is as if the electric current and the wires that connect my heart
   and my fingertips have been cut off:
The current that makes my heart pump more blood,
The current that gives me goose bumps and reassurance.
How is this treatment?
Are there medicines to be taken on a daily basis that make you feel?
Or intensive physiotherapy sessions at the hands of specialized
   doctors?
There are those who denounce my condition and accuse me of
   exaggerating when I send my complaints to them in order to
   deflect the issues.
Is there a tariff that I forgot to pay,
Or amounts and fees for this sensitive and vital service?
Surely you lose a lot when that feeling stops,
Turn into a machine
That does what is asked of it without a human reaction.
Perhaps there was a sin I committed, and the punishment was to
   be worked on.
Extensive research and investigation into the causes will not bring
   me back—the nervous impulses have leaked everywhere.
I will try to live and adapt to my condition,
But I love and adore my brown hands and fingers.
I will try to remember the feeling and take back my past actions
   with you.
I'll use it with a little acting, sometimes an exaggeration,
Until they find a cure for my condition.

# Full Stops

I always put in commas for you,
But you insist on adding full stops.
I add an arch on them, change their forms, and recreate their throne,
But you come back again, putting in the dot—
A dot and a line start.

# Balance

The balance of love is unconventional,
Informal;
It doesn't have two pans, so it is unusual.
You will not get when you give, and you will not give until
    you get.
You will give
And get,
And get
And give,
And give
And give, with no weight and balance.

## → 13 ←

# Telepathy

Whenever I say something,
I feel I have said it before.
I remember
Having spoken it to myself over and over
Before I tell you of it.

# Dilemma

Shall I uproot this perennial tree from its roots?
Shall I cut the street under my feet?
Shall I wrestle with the windmills of my heart,
Knock them down?
Or should I sit motionless
And let them defeat me?
I go back to my grey-haired notebook and write in it.
I kill the remaining years of his youth.
Shall I?

# Ascites

I am like a broad and fertile expanse of land;
You are like a farmer.
Would you own the waters to water me,
Or should I wait for the sky?
The sky is delayed,
The deserts are creeping.
It is getting hotter,
When they prayed
And the rows were lined up pray and ask God for rain,
I had fallen behind.

# Burning

What is the temperature at which the sense dies and is lost?
They say when love intensifies to a third-degree burn,
The burnt part stays as it is, but it loses its sense.
When everything is turned into *thingness*
Or the creatures become lifeless when touched.
So no difference is there between humans and stones.
I think he is alive when I see him move and hear his heartbeat,
Except that all of them are alike:
They are animate but without a soul.

# Shadow

Why didn't you tell me,
O shadow, when I disappeared beside him
That you will not hide my fragility, my fragmentation, my
brokenness?
I was about to die before I reached you.
Now, after all that,
You have hidden my handsomeness, my beauties, and uncovered
my flaws.
Sorry I didn't move from my place after sleeping:
I will be waiting over there
Until my doomsday comes.

# Our Tales

There are tales and stories
That upon hearing don't go beyond two parties,
The narrator and the listener.
When the listener is absent and it is difficult to find him, you will
    narrate the story to yourself,
And every time you tell it, you feel estrangement, and you say,
    "Did this really happen?
Or is it just a fairy tale?"
When you read my phrases, you will remember your own tales;
No doubt you will be astonished by your story,
A true story.

# The Borders

I reached the outskirts of your old life you kept guarded,
A life that loved to be within its borders.
I know not what is behind the wall;
Is it a paradise in the form of a prison,
Or custody in the form of a orchard?
At the end, you are knocking at the door of your heaven, your
  paradise, your custody and your prison.
You alone know the secrets of these borders within which the laws
  forbid my existence.
I was turned aside.
Behind you was a large board on which was written in big letters
GOODBYE.

# The Days

The days have answered my questions.
I asked a year. My answers have arrived now.
Why now?
You were late. I have been waiting for nearly a year.
You arrived when I no longer needed you.
My riddle was solved after they announced the winner
In a magazine I used to buy every morning on the date of its
    release.
I need my magazine no more;
They announced the winner.

# Travel

thought you in the homeland, within my latitude and longitude.
But no. How long would I play along with this pseudo-idea?
I saw you arranging your luggage in a line.
I saw the white-leaf book, your crossing document,
And saw
And saw
And saw
The airport officer searching among the pages of the document;
    he was turning its leaves.
Then he stopped.
He raised his head towards you.
He set his seal, shaking the world:
Exit.

# Lose

You—
Your shadow never departed you from sunrise
Until the twilight came, celebrated by the moon and the stars.
How lucky you are!
My rose was set down,
But my shadow is still lost.

# Hope

I didn't give up.
I watered a small plant and waited.
I slept,
And it grew up.
I watered it more.
Its flowers no longer grew.
I did not despair.
I waited.
I exposed it to the sun
And showed it to the moon from crescent to full.
Its branches did not move.
I didn't give up.
So don't talk to me about despair:
I haven't given up yet.

# Humans

Thus is our state, we the humans; we are thrown out because of a
  straw,
But we endure the stones.

## → 25 ←

# Proof

I requested the evidence.
I requested the proof.
I asked for a trial.
I asked one of them or less than one,
"Do you know that my request by itself is evidence, proof, and
    judgment?
Do you know that?"

# Difference

I know I am different
In my thought, my language,
My features, my love—
I'm all different.
That is why I am not surprised.

# Zero

When I believed my idea so well,
It resulted in a sin.
I wished it were true,
But supposition became disappointment.
My hopes are simple;
Poor dreams,
I asked you a thousand times, you answered me with a zero.

# Weak Link

"The chain"
My position among them does not matter,
But I do not wish to be weaker than them.
Suddenly the weak one breaks.
That's when you know,
But
Too late.
Until the chain broke and scattered,
You don't know who you are,
Unfortunately.

# Ambiguity

Smoke escapes to the source of light,
he breathes that vapor that rises between them
So that he does not get lost in the darkness, forgetting the way
   back.
He often does not return.
Smoke escapes to every bright and well-lit place,
Flees from the flame to the unknown.
You do not know that the flame, despite its hotness,
Is better than the mysterious blackness,
And I'm vague,
Inflamed,
And unknown.

# Beginning

I'm no longer among your possessions.
Some of them fell on the road.
Someone will find me and rob me, or hand me over to a place
   where trusts are deposited.
All that is valuable is often lost and never returned.
Even if you come back,
I'll start over.

## ❯ 31 ❮

# Drowning

We live and wander in the drops of the known,
But the sea of the unseen is wider and greater.
We seek to reach the shores, and we drown.

# Busy

There are things that occupy my mind, and they are among the
    things that deserve this preoccupation.
It is inevitably a heavy load,
But its weight is the size of a feather when you arrive.

# Novel

I was sitting on that wooden chair, and my eyes were reading a
  novel.
My mind was reading another narrative,
A novel whose first pages began more than a year ago.
I put the book back in its place safely.
My mind is still reading my novel,
A book with many pages between its covers.
I tore them apart
And inserted among them new papers.

# Death

Every letter I wrote has the spirit inside me,
And when I took him out of my depths,
I wrote in the folds of paper,
*Navigate to the mercy of God!*

# Revenge

I stayed in space too long
Without gravity.
My feet haven't touched solid ground in a long time
And here I am, my feet standing on my ground again.
I will need some time to be able to walk,
And after that time I will never look at the sky again.
I will let the sky, to take my revenge.

# The Battlements

I know I may have practiced the most powerful methods of
   torture with you,
But why do you think?
Did you ask me or yourself about the reasons?
I'll tell you. Let me tell you.
Imagine one who used to live in the luxury of paradise but
   suddenly finds himself in the battlements between heaven and
   hell.
What do you expect his reaction to be?
He used to live near you, share your details and your life,
Then became like a stranger looking for a chance to talk to you.
Do you know the condition of an addict when his opium is kept
   from him?
Agitate, explode, and break everything around him, starting with
   himself.
For this addiction I don't want to be treated and cured; I want it
   to be complete.
Even if I die from an overdose of you
I will love you
And love you more.

# Scream

When the tongue is unable to express,
The letters on the keyboard are similar.
I write, and it goes without an address.
It is understood without its meaning.
My love is well understood;
Longing is misunderstood.
Waiting is understood as regret.
I'm afraid to write;
I am afraid to explode in anger in public,
And I am afraid that he will not read the unwritten.
When I wrote,
I didn't want to leave anything for interpretation.
I was asking,
"Why do I pass judgment?"
I know, I'm writing.
Then I erased. Then I wrote. Then I erased.
And that's what's left,
Even if I judged and wronged,
Because I wanted to hear you scream, "I will love you as long as I
    live!"
I'm not trying to change your mind.
Whatever you decide, nothing will change inside me.
*I love you.*

# Memorial

Why did you all agree with me?
What have I done to you?
Whenever I run away from another corner, I find him.
Crumbs are enough to remind you of food.
I run away from my mind, throwing it between the pages of
    books.
I go out to my street and find its drawings scattered on my
    sidewalks and on people's faces!
Whenever I run away from a corner, I throw it in another corner.
One of the letters of his name suffices, a scene that represents my
    situation with him:
Poems of Ibn Abd al-Muhsin,
A child's laughter,
A piece of candy that you used to eat.
There is nothing left.
Everything,
Everything,
Everything …

# Future

May I have two or three space hours?
There is an hour in space, and years on earth, so I can see how
my situation will be!

# Hours

My daily hours are different from others'.
I have only twenty-two hours in my day,
And the time left is no longer mine—
Or maybe the other way around!

## ⇥ 41 ⇤

# Wonder

The lips were silenced, and the stone spoke.

# Change

Mountains moved,
And the foot was unable to.
The liars believed, and the news was false.

⟶ 43 ⟵

# Transition

Today I was sitting on the runway in the airport of the Hereafter,
Sand and soil.
Witnesses border it from the right and the left, so that the plane
    landed safely.
I was in the cemetery.
Even when you arrive for no reason—might be great love—
It could be the end.

# Letters

What I have written, poetry or prose, makes you come to me,
    crawling or running;
Makes you come to me, begging that I hear you.
And when I hear you, if you accept that,
Look me in the eye to make sure I'm completely convinced of
    what you said,
Dispelling atoms of doubt,
One atom,
One atom,
One atom.
*The lips were silenced, and the stone spoke.*
I will not write to you again.
All the next letters are not yours.
It's just me.
End of story!

→ 45 ←

# Repetition

I live my story and my day with multiple scenarios—
The same facts, the same events, the same time,
But with a change of main characters!

# Autumn Leaf

My features are beautiful.
My look is harsh, and the tan is my color.
But at any moment I am broken and crumble, like her.

# Fall

Rain, tears—
Where can I cry profusely?
Come down, please, rain. I will get wet with your pouring drops
    and my tears.
My eyes are narrowed down on the world
As the streets and avenues narrow in on me.
And if it doesn't rain, I won't wait.
I will cry tears and scream.
I will not be patient;
I will not be patient any longer.
The time for rain has come.

# Beginner

The ceremonies of the end are the beginning.

The ceremonies are as close as they can be to a funeral when the deceased is significant.

We are humble and may disappear to the one who has nothing to do with him.

Do you know where you are, in which frame to put it?

Or are you still waiting?

They have thrown dust upon me without consolation!

"It wasn't me; it was him,.

For they witnessed my birth in another dimension.

# Addiction

I got addicted to writing.
I started with a few letters,
But the dose is no longer enough for me.
I'm addicted to that feeling that ends with a dot.
I lose desire when I write a lot.
Should I stop and start taking the medication?
My pens are ready, and my pages are pure white.
Shall I stop?

# Stop

"Stop!"
It's like something saying to me.
"Stop, stop!"
A message on a clear board without introductions:
*Stop!*
It was not satisfied with my language only, but its languages were
  many.
To assure me the act of standing,
I stood up for a while.
Then I found someone else telling me,
"Stop!"

# Fingers

I woke up from my sleep, and my heart was overflowing with
  feelings.
I didn't know why!
When I looked at my hand, I remembered:
I was holding on to it when she visited me in a dream.
I felt his fingers touching my hands.
I don't think it's a dream.
She was definitely with me in one of the dimensions we live in
  without knowing it.
She left that feeling to me and went.
How I love her fingers that get lost in my hand!

# Fossil

I remember your picture:

The one you gave me, or I took without your knowledge. The
important thing is,

Did you know that I did not remove it from the place where I
put it?

In my imagination of you, there are thousands of images,

So there is no need to get them out of their hiding places!

# Absence

You are my partner who, whenever I am alone with myself,
    crowds out all inanimate objects:
My book, my pen, my clothes, and my watch.
Share them, impose your presence!
And when you're late, they will go to you and tell you about my
    condition:
*I am available.*
They can't stand your absence, so what about me?

# One Side

Love starts from one side,
And when it finishes, one of the parties, just one of them,
Continues to love
Because true love never fails.
Stay forever.

# Forcemeat

You know that everyone who wrote a letter to you
Has hidden lines and pages,
And this letter was not written voluntarily
But despite the words of its owner.

# New

At the beginning of this New Year,
To be positive I will tell you, *I am desperate.*

# Stage

Despair is a beautiful condition,
A stage on which you announce that your powers have fallen
And the hour of rest has come.

# It Might Be the Last

I will open all the doors I closed for you.
My door was hermetically closed to you,
But I will open it for everyone who knocks.
There are doors that have not been knocked on, and that's okay:
The exemption will also include them.

# Gifts

He gave me a pen. How much I loved that pen!
His last gift was the pen. Did I hold it to try it out?
Did you write down some words with it?
In your imagination, I'm the one who catches it as it wanders the
   stretchy white fields.
Who will tell me now that you are gone?
That is why I decided to turn that belief into a reality, and from
   today I write in your handwriting.

# Exception

I am looking for a newspaper that reaches all parts of the world.
Not only can my people read it, although it is not written in my
     language,
But it reaches all humans—with the exception of him, that is.

# Crossroads

This book of mine will guide you to a crossroads,
You can choose whatever road you want:
One, draws a smile on your lips, when I know how honest my
feelings were;
Another, makes you feel ashamed and disgraced because you lost
something irreplaceably precious;
The last way, will make you strive to change everything that was
written on his simple pages.
Now that I have written to you, start writing to me!

# My Perfume

How nice it is to hug yourself!
You put your favorite cologne on your winter jacket and cuddled it
    in this freezing cold.
No one will accuse you of having a different fragrance on your
    breath
Because you were hugging yourself.

# My Birthday

How can I cross out this last year of my life now?
I couldn't repeat the classes and materials that year; they were
    counted.
The proof of that is my birth certificate, which was issued on one
    of the days of February.

# Access

He did not give me a reason or a simple way to intercede for his
    sins.
This is what he meant: *I think so.*
All his attitudes and the words he did not utter attested to that.
He wanted to reach the result without looking at the method,
In the end he arrived...

# Door

I was walking that day in one of the neighborhoods.
When I stopped, there was a wooden door standing next to me.
Will my door also be this close?
Is it one step away, or one turn around?

# Far Away

Nothing will satisfy me
Except feeling that you are a worthless being when you see me
    from afar,
Because I will stay away from you as long as I live.
I will live until after my death,
And as for you, you died when you missed my birthday.

# Survival

This is the one memory I have left: she is the best I have known in
    my life.
It remains and does not go away no matter what happens,
And you will stay.

# Wound

I did not know the form of your presence in the details of my life.
Was it balm,
Or a wound deep inside me?
Was the feeling of coldness that passes through my body from
    your specter, which comes and goes without an appointment?
Or was it from the effect of the winds touching the blood from
    that wound?

# Consolation

When the beautiful scents of happiness come, I remember you,
And when storms of sorrow and unhappiness blow,
I remember you too...

# Combination

Love is a combination medicine:
It turns into a deadly poison if they make a mistake in its
   composition.

# Injustice

In one of your letters, you wrote to me, *Stop oppressing me.*
And I tell you that the silence you practice is one of the dearest
     friends of injustice; rather, it belongs to the same slackness.
I also write to you: *You have oppressed me in all calm and silence!*

# Revival

I will search for your likeness in my vast world full of human
  beings.
I will suffice with the milestones and distinguish marks
I'll hit one of them or stumble for sure.
I will look for the forty who were created resembling you.
I will search to revive your memory

# Brick

Have you ever asked yourselves about the armed battle that every writer fights, wielding his sword?

He fights every critic and attacker who harms his production and creativity, written or published.

Did you ask?

This is because you see a pile of lines and letters.

But he sees, lives, and breathes, kidnapped his breath, which resides in his papers to write and delete, wipe and cut, and leads back down to reach the conclusion that ends in your hands.

And you, all you care about, is looking for the missing brick.

# Dedication

To everyone whose bride is absent from her wedding,
To everyone whose character was left out of his book,
I dedicate these phrases:
Who has issued his book and sat at the book-signing event,
    waiting?

# Fact

Every little lie hides behind a bigger truth,
But what does the great lie hide?

→ 76 ←

# Appearance

How much of myself has appeared to the public?
Does mystery still cover me?
Or my words revealed, and stripped me of my weapons,
which I did not originally own?

# Reality

I tell my story with you to the children, for no one else is listening,
As if it is one of the fairy tales and you resemble Cinderella, Snow
    White, and Alice—
Until I believed myself that you are a fictional character
Told in stories,
Living in books,
Perished when setting foot on the ground.

# Whiff

*To my perfume*

Who owned the keys to my hidden doors?
A small whiff is enough to open a door, or all at once.

# Silence

Time will pass, and when they I you, I'll tell you:
You have changed. I no longer know you.
You are no longer the person that I know
We have met, But I didn't say
You didn't tell...

# Search

I would like to give you something that does not wear out or
    perish,
Does not die and does not dry up,
Something that lasts forever.
I didn't find that thing.
I wanted to give my love, but this thing is not given,I don't own it.
I didn't find that thing:
I'm still searching.

# Stoppage

I remember when I was young,

I was taken, and I ran away from my friend so as not to be caught and beaten because I had displeased him.

I remember saying, "That's Ok, I will stop, and I am ready to take the punishment that you choose."

I cannot run;

I grew tired.

I am tired.

This is my situation now!

# A Stranger

If estrangement were a profession, I would be at the top of it.
No one else will jostle with me or stand in the queue ahead of me.
I am a stranger, and this is my profession:
I had the honor of knowing you.

# Cruelty

The lover does not know how to harden,
If he does, or made it up, it will not be long, only for a few
moments, and he will return to his love.
The cruel person, no matter he claims love, will remain the rock
opposed. No matter how planted and irrigated, the seeds will
not be reached by the water but be frozen and petrified like
the owner, and the water will flow up to the bottom.
A seed that was buried may sprout within the confines of that
rock. As for the rock, it will remain hard.

# Stagnation

Love stops the wheel of life,
Stops the clock;
Everything stops winding
And in that rotation
Everything revolves around it.

# Words

When I talk about honesty, these were the most honest moments,
And when I talk about staying, the pages stay with me much more
    than their owner.
I spent hours and days with her, writing to her and them,
And she promises me even now that she will stay with me forever.

# Flames

Has the heat of the forty-degree weather changed?
Have the landmarks and terrain changed? Or am I the one who
has lost the feeling and sensation of weather and the heat?
Or is there something stronger and greater within me than that
weather?

# Strength of Weakness

Many of us are unaware, as we write a simple sentence in a blog,
that we have thus been recognized as weak. Has life made
him tired?
You will undoubtedly find recognition between those lines.
But at the same time, it is a great power to confess and reveal his
pure spirit.
He who writes like me will understand and express.

# Recovery

Exposure to cruelty is a treatment that does not convey to you the
   distress a person suffers from but rather gives you a dose to
   continue and rise quickly.
And when you fall, your recovery time is shortened.
In the past, I might need months, but now!
The period of recovery is not mentioned.
You do not remember how
To go back to the way you were, and sometimes better and
   stronger,
But an version of yourself is updating.

# Fall

Love stories are devoid of lessons and exhortations. They are
    completely empty,
Because no matter how many trials you go through, you will fall
    again into the same pit, thinking, *This was someone,*
And out of fear of doing wrong to him,
You will end up unjust to yourself.
It's the truth.

# Mistake

Is there anything harder than stone?
Yes, it's the heart.

→ 91 ←

# Where

If you are all of the oppressed, then where are the unjust in the
story?

# Heartbeat

Someone asked me one day, "Will you write a book for me as you
    wrote for others?"
I don't know if he wanted me or the book!
The strange thing is that he could not bear to read a single page
    of my book to him.
He was frightened by the sound of my heartbeat rising between its
    lines and ran away.
But If you want the book, you can gift it to yourself; it is the same
    as my old book.
I am certain that its pages have been gifted to many other than its
    owner,
And are still gifted.

# Let down

What if there was a logo or illustration for each situation?
Let's start with "letting down" as an example.
What is the most appropriate picture?
Do you think drowning in an inch of water is sufficient? Or is it
a picture of a person who has lost his sight while at the top of
his happiness, or …

# Plurality

I thought the poem was written for one person only.
I did not expect that it might be given to anyone other than him,
Until this day came.

# Receptor

Feeling receptors may be absent in one of the limbs,
So do not be surprised when you do not understand your words,
  your feelings, and all your actions.
If that receiver is absent, then everything you do is in vain.
It is normal that when sending those frequencies and waves
You do not understand them, because the receptors do not exist.

# Finished

The first manifestation of love is to write to the one you love, and the last of it is also.

# Exchange

When the lips are silent about the truth, the number of dumb
devils increases.
But the devil must encounter another devil, so he will be silent
about the truth of the first.
Amen.

# Debt

To everyone who helps an oppressor, know that they will
    inevitably defeat you.
It won't be long.
You don't have to wait long,
I promise you.
As for me,
I will pray to God for that time to draw near. Amen.

# Complete

The strangest moments of longing
To make your heart beat with joy:
When you mention your poem you left incomplete in the corner of
    your place,
You come back quickly to finish what you started,
And when you arrive, you discover that it was complete:
Me.

# Honesty

Honest people are more subject to pain.

# The Legacy

I will not leave my messages or my poems scribbled within me.
I will publish them in books and newspapers.
I'll scatter them on the shelves.
I leave behind evidence of everything I've been through,
And when I am far from this world
You will have an inheritance. Take from it what you want; it is
   yours.

# Decisive

The first meeting is always decisive.

# Reminder

When roses are gifted and the owner of the gift goes,
The roses remain to remind you of him.
So I gave myself a handful of roses
To remember for myself what I have always forgotten and
neglected.
I apologize to myself.

# Relationship

In the balance of our relationship,
Tell me what you put on the scales?
Because I don't see it.
As for my balance, it is no longer a place for weighing,
Or did you put your weight on another scale?
Tell me…

# Epilogue

You are witnesses: I write to them, I mean *someone*. The range
   has covered the earth and the sky I write to them.
My mind was stolen: you are the witnesses.
My heart I posted briefly on my page: he read my handwriting
   and understood.
You are the witnesses.
That was before. My situation now has changed. I have no one but
   paper. I write to you on my page; it is the same, and you are
   the witnesses.
I am the end.

Printed in the United States
by Baker & Taylor Publisher Services